# EARVIN "MAGIC" JOHNSON

# EARVIN "MAGIC" JOHNSON

## Champion and Crusader
### by Ted Gottfried

A Book Report Biography
FRANKLIN WATTS
A Division of Grolier Publishing
New York / London / Hong Kong / Sydney
Danbury, Connecticut

Cover illustration by James Mellett, interpreted from photographs by © Allsport USA/Stephen Dunn, and Liaison Agency, Inc./Barry King.

Photographs ©: AllSport USA: cover background, 13, 83 (Stephen Dunn), 23 (Bruce Hazelton), 79 (Ken Levine), 95; AP/Wide World Photos: 89 (Ed Bailey), 103 (Joe Brockert), 97 (Michael Caulfield), 107 (The Cleveland Plain Dealer/Chuck Crow), 110 (Al Goldis), 70 (Lennox McLendon), 91 (Chris O'Meara), 17 (Susan Ragan), 31, 41; Corbis-Bettmann: 77 (Mitchell Gerber), 35, 38, 43, 44, 48, 74; Icon Sports Media: 2, 15 (John McDonough); Liaison Agency, Inc.: cover foreground (Barry King); NBA Photos: 50, 60, 71, 109 (Andrew D. Bernstein), 88 (Nathaniel S. Butler), 29, 56 (Peter Read Miller); Sports Illustrated Picture Collection: 90, 98, 100 (Andrew D. Bernstein), 65 (Steve Lopofski), 19 (John McDonough).

Visit Franklin Watts on the Internet at:
http://publishing.grolier.com

Library of Congress Cataloging-in-Publication Data

Gottfried, Ted.
Earvin "Magic" Johnson : champion and crusader / by Ted Gottfried.
    p.  cm.—(Book report biography)
Includes bibliographical references and index.
ISBN 0-531-11675-1 (lib. bdg.)   0-531-15550-1 (pbk.)
    1. Johnson, Earvin, 1959—Juvenile literature. 2. Basketball players—United States—Biography—Juvenile literature. [1. Johnson, Earvin, 1959– 2. Basketball players. 3. Afro-Americans—Biography.] I. Title. II. Series.

GV884.J63 G68 2001
796.323'092—dc21
[B]                                            00-038195

## DEDICATION

For computer wizard Rudy Kornmann—with much gratitude

## ACKNOWLEDGMENTS

I am most grateful to my son Dan Gottfried and to my stepson-in-law Rudy Kornmann for their time, help, and expertise in building my new computer and dealing with its program glitches. I am also grateful to my old friend Ken Schwartzman for his basketball expertise and advice in writing this book. Many thanks to the personnel of the New York Central Research Library, the Donnell Library Center, the central branch of the Queens-boro Public Library, and especially the Epiphany Branch Library. Finally—with much love—I want to acknowledge the contribution of my wife, Harriet Gottfried, who, as always, read and critiqued this book. Her help was invaluable.

# CONTENTS

# EARVIN "MAGIC" JOHNSON

# CHAPTER ONE

## MAGIC IS A SOMETIME THING

An old saying among professional athletes goes like this: "Sometimes the magic works. Sometimes it doesn't." This saying summarizes the life of Magic Johnson. When he was recruited out of college by the Los Angeles Lakers to begin his professional basketball career, the magic was working. When a knee injury at the start of his second season with the Lakers kept him out of forty-five consecutive games, the magic wasn't working.

When Magic and the Lakers won the 1985 National Basketball Association (NBA) championship over the Boston Celtics and arch rival Larry Bird, the magic was working. But the year before, when Bird and the Celtics snatched the championship from Magic and the Lakers in a seven-game series, it wasn't working. When Magic scored twenty-five points in the 1992 All-Star Game and was named Most Valuable Player, the magic was working. But a few months earlier, when he tested positive for **HIV**—the virus that causes **AIDS**—the magic seemed to have abandoned him.

## THE DREAM TEAM

HIV changed Magic's life. Before he learned that he was infected, Magic Johnson had racked up one of the all-time-great career records in professional basketball. He had played in 874 games over 12 seasons to score a total of 17,239 points, giving him a career average of 19.7 points a game. He had a 52 percent **field goal** record and had scored 85 percent of his **free throws**. He had a total of 6,376 **rebounds** and 1,698 **steals** to his credit. As for **assists**, his career total of 10,141 is second only to that of John Stockton. Along with Kareem Abdul-Jabbar, Larry Bird, and Michael Jordan, Magic Johnson is rated one of the greatest basketball players ever.

Magic was already committed to play in the 1992 All-Star Game when he learned he was **HIV positive** and announced his retirement. He also had another commitment. He had been selected to play on the 1992 Olympic basketball team. It was called the Dream Team. Magic Johnson, Larry Bird, Patrick Ewing, Charles Barkley, and

*Earvin "Magic" Johnson is one of the greatest
basketball players of all time.*

Michael Jordan were among those chosen to rep-
resent the United States in the Olympics.
Sportswriters said it was the greatest basketball
team ever assembled.

## FEEDING THE BIRD

The U.S. players had all played against one another in the past. They had been rivals—sometimes bitter rivals—but now they were teammates. Playing guard, Magic was thrilled to look across the court and see Michael Jordan as the other guard. It was also a kick to be named co-captain of the Olympic team along with Larry Bird—his archenemy on the court and his good friend off it.

In the practice sessions, Olympic coach Chuck Daly always put Magic and Michael Jordan on opposite teams. Watching Jordan with his inside moves, soaring leaps to the hoop, and **slam dunks**, Magic concluded that Jordan was the best player in the game. But when the Dream Team played its first game against Cuba, it was Magic and Larry Bird who earned extravagant praise from the sportswriters covering the game.

The Olympic game against Cuba was the first time Magic and Bird had been on the same side, but they worked together as smoothly as if they'd been teammates for years. Magic kept feeding Larry the ball, and Larry kept dropping it in the basket. Some of those who watched the game said their teamwork was as graceful as a well-rehearsed ballet.

*The 1992 U.S. Olympic Dream Team was considered the best basketball team ever assembled. It included superstars such as Patrick Ewing, Scottie Pippen, Michael Jordan, Larry Bird, Magic Johnson, and Charles Barkley.*

## AN HIV CELEBRITY

The 1992 Summer Olympics were held in Barcelona, Spain, and the Dream Team was competing against the world's best players. Many opponents were professionals in their own countries. To the opposing teams and their fans, Magic was a celebrity. He realized that his retirement from professional basketball—and the reason for it—had affected people far beyond the borders of the United States. For the most part, the response was sympathetic. Often, it was mixed with admiration.

It had taken guts to stand up and admit to the world that he was carrying the AIDS virus. Whenever Magic left his hotel in Barcelona he was mobbed with requests for autographs. Even players on the opposing teams wanted a souvenir after they played against him. Every member of the Dream Team was a celebrity, but Magic was now regarded as quite special.

## BRINGING HOME THE GOLD

The Dream Team won the last game of the 1992 Olympics against the Croatian squad—117 to 85. The Americans had won all eight games. The average point spread between them and the eight losing teams was 43.7. The average score was 117 to 73.

They brought home the gold! In his autobiography, *My Life*, Magic would write of the "magnificent moment" when they were awarded the Olympic gold medal. He almost broke down during the "Star Spangled Banner." It was a memory he would always cherish—the high point of a life that began thirty-three years earlier in a small midwestern city not far from Detroit, Michigan.

*Magic cherishes the moment he received an Olympic gold medal for basketball in 1992.*

# CHAPTER TWO

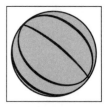

## JUNE BUG HOOPIN'

Earvin Johnson Jr. was born on August 14, 1959, in Lansing, Michigan. He was the fourth of seven children born to Earvin Johnson Sr. and his wife, Christine. The family also included three children from Earvin Sr.'s previous marriage. Earvin Jr., who would one day be known throughout the sports world as "Magic," never lacked playmates.

The Johnsons were not rich, but they didn't live in poverty either. They squeezed into a yellow frame house with three small bedrooms on the second floor. Magic's parents had one bedroom. His four sisters—Pearl, Kim, and the twins, Evelyn and Yvonne—shared the second. Magic bunked with his two older brothers, Quincy and Larry.

Magic's father worked full time in a General Motors factory. With so many mouths to feed, he also held two part-time jobs. Clearly, he didn't have much time to relax. However, every Sunday afternoon, Earvin Sr. watched the NBA basketball games on TV.

## A BASKETBALL FAMILY

The Johnsons were a basketball family. Magic's father had played basketball in high school. His mother had also played basketball when she was younger. Both of his older brothers played too. Earvin Sr. explained the basics of the game to his children. Growing up, as Magic and his brother

*Magic's parents, Earvin and Christine Johnson*

Larry developed their skills, their father often discussed the fine points of the game with them.

"Dad made me see the importance of the little things in basketball," Magic recalled in later years.

**"Dad made me see the importance of the little things in basketball."**

Growing up wasn't all basketball for Magic, though. His father worked hard and expected his sons to do the same. First they had chores around the house, and then they had outside jobs. Everybody in the Johnson family had to pull his or her weight.

From the time he was big enough to carry a rake, Magic cleaned the yard, raked the leaves, and shoveled snow from the driveway. As he grew older, he mowed lawns and cleared snow for the neighbors. He also helped his father on one of his part-time jobs, cleaning oil and grease from garage floors.

## DREAMS AND DETERMINATION

In one of Magic's part-time jobs, he cleaned the offices of two successful African-American businessmen. When his work was finished, he liked to sit behind an impressive executive desk, put his feet up, and pretend he was the boss giving orders. "'Do this! Take care of that!' I'd imagine that everybody in the whole building worked for me, and that I had the respect of the entire town," Magic remembered.

Lansing, where Magic lived, was mainly a white community. The blacks who lived there did not have much money. Like Magic's family, most had to struggle to make ends meet. The two successful African-American businessmen were the exceptions. They had large, beautiful homes and drove expensive, late-model cars. In a way, they were an inspiration to Magic. He decided that an African-American man could make it if he really tried, and Magic was determined to try.

**"I'd imagine that everybody in the whole building worked for me, and that I had the respect of the entire town."**

## DRIBBLE, DRIBBLE, DRIBBLE

Whatever Magic did, he kept at it until he got it right. He never quit. When he was very small, he would dribble a ball on the sidewalk in front of his house for hours. Soon he was dribbling everywhere he went. When Magic carried groceries for his mother, he dribbled with his free hand. On his way to school, he balanced his books and switched them from hand to hand as he dribbled.

As a little boy he was chubby, showing no sign that he would grow up to be 6 feet 9 inches (206 centimeters) tall, but that didn't stop Magic. He spent hours at the Main Street School playground practicing **layups**—shots from near the basket usually made by playing the ball off the backboard. Because he was small and round, the neighbors nicknamed him "June Bug." Passing him at the playground as the sun went down, they'd say, "There goes that crazy June Bug, hoopin' all day."

> **"There goes that crazy June Bug, hoopin' all day."**

## A JUNIOR-HIGH STAR

When Magic was eight years old, he began playing **one-on-one** against his brother Larry. Besides being a year older, Larry was bigger and stronger. But all those hours of dribbling paid off for Magic. Superior strength was no match for speed and agility, and Magic ran his brother ragged.

Soon Magic began to grow. His baby fat just seemed to melt away. By eighth grade he was 6 feet 4 inches (193 cm) tall. He had been playing junior-high basketball for a couple of years, and people were beginning to notice him. It was no big deal to Magic—it was fun; it was just a game.

His father saw it differently, however. Earvin Sr. was a huge basketball fan. His favorite player was Wilt Chamberlain. He liked to watch Kareem Abdul-Jabbar, Bill Russell, and other

*When Magic was young, he and his father enjoyed watching basketball stars such as Kareem Abdul-Jabbar.*

great basketball stars with his sons. He pointed out their offensive and defensive strategies to the boys, and later, when he watched Magic play junior-high ball, he could see that his son had paid attention. He also saw something else. He saw that Magic could be not just a good basketball player, but a *great* basketball player.

In junior high, Magic's team won the Lansing city championship two years in a row. Both times Magic was the high scorer. He couldn't wait to move on to Sexton High School, a nearby all-black school that was famous for its championship basketball teams.

## A BIG BLACK DOT

Magic never went to Sexton High School. In the 1970s, integration required that many children be bused to different schools. Magic was bused to Everett High School, a mainly white school on the other side of town.

He was furious. Everett's basketball team, the Vikings, had one of the worst records in the state of Michigan. People said that they couldn't run, couldn't jump, couldn't sink baskets, and couldn't win. Magic's brother, Larry, had gone to Everett the year before and had made the basketball team, only to be thrown off it after an argument with the coach.

Magic was truly miserable. Busing was still relatively new at Everett High, and African-American kids were not exactly welcome there. The year before, when Larry was one of the first blacks to be bused in, rocks had been thrown at him and the other black students. Even now, the small group of blacks and the large group of whites did not mingle. Magic remembers that at basketball games, "the black kids all sat together under the basket, like a big black dot on a white page."

**"The black kids all sat together under the basket, like a big black dot on a white page."**

## FRICTION ON THE COURT

In spite of his feelings, Magic tried out for the Everett basketball team. He made the team, but on the first day of practice, it was painfully obvious to him that the white players didn't want a black on their team. "My teammates froze me out," he remembers.

**"My teammates froze me out," he remembers. "Time after time I was wide open, but nobody threw me the ball."**

"Time after time I was wide open, but nobody threw me the ball."

Magic got mad. The next time he got his hands on the ball, he drove down the court all by himself and jammed it through the hoop. He repeated the maneuver until one of the white players demanded that he pass the ball instead of taking all the shots himself. They almost came to blows, but the team coach—George Fox—got between them and prevented the boys from fighting.

Fox was the first coach to realize that Magic played most effectively as a **point guard**. He was the tallest player on the team and normally would have been assigned to play forward or center while the smaller boys worked the ball down the court into shooting position. But Magic had spent years practicing ball handling, and his father had trained him to read the defense. He could make the split-second decisions needed to get the ball to an open teammate. Coach Fox broke with tradition and made the most of Magic's skills.

## MUTT AND JEFF

Soon the white players accepted Magic. Their performance as a team was improving, and they knew his contribution was largely responsible for that. The door was now open for other African-American boys to join the team, and some of them were very good. The team was beginning to turn into championship material.

Prejudice hadn't been overcome, however. When three African-American girls tried out for the cheerleading squad, they were not chosen—even though they were obviously better than some of the white girls. Magic organized the black players on the team to boycott practice in protest. As a result, black girls were added to the cheerleading squad for the first time in the history of Everett High School.

One of the African-Americans who made the basketball team was Reggie Chastine. Like Magic, he had been bused to Everett High to integrate blacks into the traditionally all-white student body. He was 5 feet 3 inches (160 cm) tall—the smallest player on the team. A year ahead of Magic in school, he was a whiz at handling the ball. He had a knack for providing the assists necessary to set up shots. Soon he and Magic were functioning like a well-oiled machine, with Reggie feeding Magic many of the passes that made him the top scorer. The two boys also became close friends off the court. Around school they were known as Mutt and Jeff, after the tall and short friends in the comic strip of the same name.

## CURING A SWELLED HEAD

By the time he was fifteen years old, Magic was a familiar and popular figure around Everett High. Having almost reached his full height of 6 feet 9 inches (206 cm), he was hard to miss in the school hallways. He may have been known on the basketball court for his wizard's hands, but in school it was his warm, friendly smile that won over his fellow students.

Around this time, local sportswriters began to focus on him. In December 1974, Fred Stabley Jr., a sportswriter for the *Lansing State Journal*, decided that Johnson was nothing less than "magic" on the basketball court. The nickname stuck.

So much attention at a young age gave Magic something of a swelled head. He began goofing off at practice and not showing up for drills. He kidded around when he should have been paying attention to new plays, strategies, and formations, and he laughed off criticism. Finally, Coach Fox had to set him straight. "Earvin," he said, "if you come tomorrow with the same attitude, and practice the same way, you won't start the next game."

Magic knew the coach meant it. "That was my wake-up call," he remembers. "I never had another problem like that throughout high school, col-

*The nickname "Magic" created an image that started in high school and lasted through Johnson's professional career.*

lege, or the pros." He learned that how well he played in a game depended directly on how seriously he worked at the drills, practice sessions, and strategy meetings before the game began.

## BORN TO BE A SPARTAN

People in Michigan take high school basketball very seriously. It was a great honor for Magic when, in his junior year at Everett High, he was chosen as Michigan's Prep Player of the Year by United Press International. He was also named All Conference Most Valuable Player. Sportswriters selected him as one of the top five high school basketball players in the United States.

It was time for Magic to start thinking about college. He was already getting invitations from colleges that were eager to have him play on their basketball team. By his senior year, the pressure to decide on a college was becoming more and more intense. Local fans in Lansing were urging him to go to Michigan State and play for the Spartans. His father was pushing for Michigan State too. He always followed the Spartans and rooted for them, and Magic had followed in his footsteps. Magic had cheered on the Spartans of Michigan State throughout his childhood.

Magic received many tempting offers, but in

the end he followed his heart to Michigan State. "I don't think I could have gone anywhere else," he told reporters at a press conference. "I was born to be a Spartan."

*Magic Johnson as a Michigan State University Spartan in 1979*

# CHAPTER THREE

# A COLLEGE STAR

Magic Johnson was eighteen years old when he arrived at Michigan State, but he was already famous. Television and newspapers had made his face known to basketball fans everywhere. He had become a celebrity while he was still in high school, and his reputation had preceded him to college.

The basketball season hadn't even started yet, but Magic's fellow students greeted him by name and asked his opinion about the Spartans' chances in the upcoming season. They were pinning their hopes on Magic. It was a heavy load for the young freshman to carry.

Central Michigan was the Spartans' first opponent that season. It was a home game, and Magic felt the pressure. The day before the game he had stomach cramps that kept him up all night. He was groggy from lack of sleep when he and his teammates jogged onto the court.

His entire family and many friends were there to see his first game for the Spartans. They were all rooting for him, but it didn't help. He missed shot after shot, and the ball was taken away from him time after time. "I really stunk up the gym," Magic admits. The Spartans won the game, but their highly anticipated new star had lost some of his luster.

## THE SPARTAN COACH

Magic soon learned that there were some big differences between high school basketball and college basketball. In high school, Magic had been famous for his jumping. He had developed a habit of jumping, just to throw the other team off balance. Sometimes he'd fake shots. Sometimes he'd jump just for the heck of it. Sometimes he'd jump and shoot. But he always thought that his spectacularly high leaps were a worthwhile distraction. And he knew the spectators loved them.

Spartan coach Jud Heathcoate let him know that players at the college level were too savvy to fall for that kind of showboating. He pointed out that while Magic was jumping, his opponents would be guarding his teammates. There would be no open receiver to take a pass from Magic. He'd end up being forced to take a bad shot—and probably while he was off balance. "Stay on the ground," the coach told him. "Nothing good can happen when you're in the air."

Jud Heathcoate was a tough coach. The Spartans were part of the Big Ten Conference, and the schools they played included many of the best players in college basketball. Heathcoate was tough on his players because the competition was so tough. He yelled at Magic and his teammates constantly. If they didn't measure up, he exploded. He had no patience with excuses, and he didn't care whether his players liked him or not. He only cared that they performed well.

Magic respected Heathcoate—but at times he felt as if he hated him. Sometimes though, hating Coach Heathcoate helped Magic's game. "I'd get mad at Jud, and then I'd take out my anger on the other team," Magic wrote in his autobiography. But he knew the coach cared only about winning, "and I was the same way."

> **"I'd get mad at Jud, and then I'd take out my anger on the other team."**

## A TEAM PLAYER

Thanks to Coach Heathcoate, the Spartans always had a good team. But until Magic joined them, they had never been described as a great team. The season before he came to Michigan

State, the Spartans had won only ten of the seventeen games they played. Despite his unimpressive first game, Magic led the way to improving the Spartans' record. His first season ended with the Spartans winning the Big Ten Conference for the first time in nineteen years.

Magic scored an average of seventeen points a game that season. But it wasn't just the points he scored that made him the acknowledged leader of the team. He was a team player, and his record on assists and rebounds earned him rare

*Magic, number thirty-three, drives to the basket as a freshman for Michigan State.*

praise from Coach Heathcoate. At the Big Ten championship press conference, the coach, not known for singling out players for praise, spoke about Magic: "You don't talk about the points he scores, but the points he produces."

**"You don't talk about the points he scores, but the points he produces."**

That year, Magic was the only freshman named to an All-American team; he would play against teams from the former Soviet Union and other countries. The end of the season brought a mailbag full of offers from professional basketball teams that wanted Magic to play for them.

### OFFERS FROM THE PROS

The offers were surely tempting. One team offered to pay him $250,000 a season for six seasons. That would be small potatoes compared to what Magic would eventually earn but, back then, to a young man from a family that had always had to struggle, it seemed like a fortune. Still, it wasn't just the money that tempted Magic. "It was finally realizing the dream of being a professional."

**"It was finally realizing the dream of being a professional."**

Opposition came from his parents, though. His mother wanted him to stay in college and graduate. His father didn't think he was ready to turn pro yet. He wanted Magic to get more experience at the college level. Magic himself felt an obligation to Michigan State, to the coach, and to his teammates. He decided to stay on for the 1978–1979 season.

The season started out well enough, but in January the Spartans slacked off and were beaten in four of the six games they played. Coach Heathcoate was not happy. He made changes in the lineup. Magic was switched from guard to forward. It went against the philosophy of his first coach in high school, but Magic soon found that his new position allowed him to dribble down court and create more under-the-hoop opportunities.

## THE NCAA PLAYOFFS

Coach Heathcoate's shape-up of the team worked, and the Spartans began racking up wins. By the end of the season, they had won twenty-one games and lost only six. That put the Spartans in line to compete for the National Collegiate Athletic Association (NCAA) championship.

They had been in the running the previous season, but were eliminated early in the playoffs. This time would be different. They won the first tournament game against Lamar College of Texas, 95 to 64. In their second game, against the Louisiana State University Tigers, Magic scored twenty-four points. He also had twelve assists. The Spartans won 79 to 71. Their next win over Notre Dame put them in the semifinals.

The four teams in the semifinals were the Michigan State Spartans, the De Paul University

*Magic Johnson and Larry Bird answer questions before the 1979 college championship game that ignited a legendary rivalry between two of the greatest basketball players ever.*

Blue Demons, the University of Pennsylvania Quakers, and the Indiana State University Sycamores. They all played on the same day at the University of Utah. Michigan State beat Pennsylvania easily and Indiana State trounced De Paul. That meant the Spartans would play the Indiana State Sycamores for the NCAA championship. It also meant that Magic would square off for the first time against the player who would be his chief rival in the pros for many years. That college championship game would be the first time Magic faced Larry Bird.

## THE BIRD

Long before that first game, Magic Johnson and Larry Bird were being compared in sports circles. They were both college stars who were establishing terrific records on the basketball courts. Larry was two-and-a-half years older—a college senior while Magic was a sophomore. He had been around longer and was usually rated higher when comparisons were made. That would even out in the future when they were both in the pros.

Even so, Larry Bird would be rated by *The Kids' World Almanac of Basketball* as "pure and simply one of the greatest players ever to walk onto a basketball court." The same source would rank Magic as one of the three greatest—the other two being Michael Jordan and, of course, Larry Bird.

On the court, Bird and Magic sometimes squared off savagely, but off the court they eventually became friends. Magic regards Bird as a friend and as the best of the many top hoopsters he played against.

Magic and Bird were an even match. They were both 6 feet 9 inches (206 cm) tall, with Magic having a slight advantage at 225 pounds (102 kilograms) to Bird's 220 pounds (100 kg). They both had the ability to see the entire court while a game was being played, as well as the ability to react to its shifting patterns. These are the traits of future champions, and that's what Magic and Bird were when they met as opponents for the first time in the NCAA national championship game.

## THE NCAA CHAMPIONSHIP

Many fans viewed the NCAA championship as a one-on-one contest between Magic and Bird. Spartan coach Heathcoate, however, had no intention of playing it that way. He saw Larry Bird as the main component of a team that had won thirty-two games in a row. If he could neutralize Bird, Indiana would be leaderless and its effectiveness would crumble.

*This 1979 NCAA championship game went down in sports history because of the ultimate matchup of Bird versus Magic. The game is still played on sports channels today.*

Coach Heathcoate set up a special zone defense with Larry as the focus. Wherever he was, Spartans were all over him. Passes to Bird were blocked. He was rushed every time he tried to shoot. The zone defense tied him up in knots.

Meanwhile, not directly facing off against Bird worked well for Magic. His skill at assists fit right in with the zone defense. They were a major factor in the Spartans' 37 to 28 halftime lead. Magic also scored well in the second half, but he had gotten into foul trouble. As a result, Indiana State pulled within six points of Michigan. Then Magic settled down, and the Spartans kept control of the ball in the final moments of the game. They won 75 to 64.

The Spartans of Michigan State were the new NCAA champions! Magic had scored twenty-four points and Bird scored nineteen. Bird had almost twice as many rebounds—thirteen to Magic's seven—but Magic had ten assists to Bird's two.

## TURNING PROFESSIONAL

On the face of it, Magic had performed better than Bird, but it was Larry Bird, not Magic Johnson, who was named College Player of the Year. It was a disappointment, but Magic didn't dwell on it—he had other things on his mind. He and his family had decided that the time had come for him to turn professional.

In June 1979, Magic was first pick in the draft by the Los Angeles Lakers. Still nineteen years old, he signed a four-year contract for

*Magic celebrates Michigan State University's victory as NCAA champions. He was named the Most Valuable Player of the game.*

$500,000 a year. Meanwhile, the Boston Celtics had signed Larry Bird for $600,000 a year.

As pros, Magic and Bird were constantly being compared. Sometimes their statistics would be quoted, sometimes the styles of play would be compared, and sometimes they would face each other directly on the basketball court. Separately and together, Magic and Bird loomed over the sport of basketball and established a standard of play that all players would be measured against.

*Magic was picked by the Los Angeles Lakers in the first round of the 1979 NBA draft. Here, Magic (third from right) and the other first-round choices pose with NBA commissioner Larry O'Brien (center).*

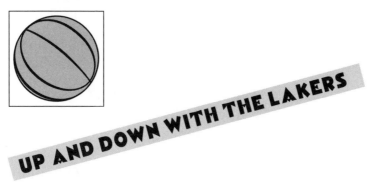

# CHAPTER FOUR

## UP AND DOWN WITH THE LAKERS

Magic's college career had skyrocketed him to the pros, but his first game with the Los Angeles Lakers found it faltering. On October 12, 1979, Magic played his first game with the Lakers against the San Diego Clippers. It was an early lesson in how rough professional basketball can be. It was a short lesson as well. Magic played for seventeen minutes and scored only one point when the coach took him out. But he went back in and by the end of the game he had twenty-six points.

He made a lot of rookie mistakes during the next few games, but he learned from them. Every now and then he made a play that brought the fans to their feet and drew fond slaps of approval from his teammates. Nobody was surprised, though, when the National Basketball Association (NBA) didn't name Magic Rookie of the Year. That

honor went to the rising star of the Boston
Celtics—Larry Bird.

## BIG BREAK

The first time Magic really lived up to his college
reputation was during the sixth game of the
1979–1980 NBA championship series. The Lakers
were in good shape. They were ahead of the
Philadelphia 76ers three games to two. One more
win and the championship was theirs. The Lakers
fans had every reason to be optimistic. So why
were they so disheartened?

The word was out that Kareem Abdul-Jabbar,
the mainspring of the team, would not be able to
play. The Lakers' star center had sprained his left
ankle in the fifth game and then sat out most of
the third period. He'd limped back out in the
fourth period and scored fourteen points. His last
basket had been a three-point shot that broke a
103–103 tie with only thirty-three seconds left to
play.

Was it any wonder that the fans adored
Abdul-Jabbar? Was it any wonder that their
hearts sank when they heard that his injured
ankle had swelled up and he was definitely out of
the sixth game? Was it any wonder that all they
could do was shake their heads sadly at the
prospect of a rookie like Magic Johnson taking the

place of the legendary Kareem Abdul-Jabbar? The general opinion was that the best Lakers fans could do was give up on game six and hope that Abdul-Jabbar would be okay in time to save the series in game seven.

## GIGGLES AND DUNKS

Magic could see those doubts in the fans' eyes. Sometimes he thought he could see them in the eyes of his teammates too. And he couldn't help having his own private doubts. After all, he hadn't played center since high school, and now he was being called on to fill the shoes of the leading center in the NBA.

When he caught a glimpse of himself in the locker-room mirror, he started to giggle. He felt like a kid pretending to be the world's greatest basketball player. He began giggling again when he took his position to wait for the **jump ball**.

The **tip-off** got away from him and the 76ers had the ball. It was not a promising start. Finally, the Lakers got it back. They scored. They racked up seven points before the 76ers began sinking baskets. The score went up and down like a see-saw after that. At halftime, the score was tied at sixty.

In the second half, the Lakers drew first blood. Magic opened with a slam dunk, and the team followed to shoot ahead by fourteen points. In the fourth period, however, the 76ers bounced back. Three times they came within one basket of tying the game. Then, with five minutes to go, the

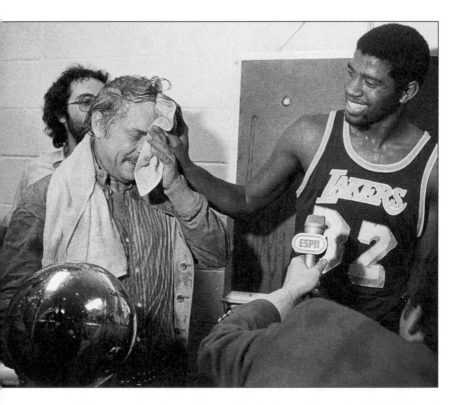

*Magic grins happily as he is interviewed with Lakers' owner Jerry Buss after winning his first NBA championship in 1980. Magic was rightfully named the series Most Valuable Player.*

Lakers caught fire. They began lobbing baskets like 2-inch (5-cm) putts on a level golf course. By the time the buzzer sounded, they'd nailed the game 123 to 107, and the Los Angeles Lakers were the NBA champions.

## DANCE, KAREEM, DANCE

For Magic, it was a personal triumph. The rookie had proved himself to the fans, to his teammates, and to his coach. He had scored an amazing forty-two points! He was credited with fifteen rebounds and seven assists. Magic

**"One of the best all-around games in the history of basketball."**

had played "one of the best all-around games in the history of basketball," according to sportswriter Rick L. Johnson (no relation to Magic). When he was named the series Most Valuable Player (MVP), everybody agreed that Magic deserved the honor.

It was an honor that everybody had thought would go to Kareem Abdul-Jabbar. Now the rookie who had replaced him snatched the MVP award away. Magic knew that must be a bitter pill for the superstar to swallow. After the MVP announcement, Magic tried to ease the hurt when he was

*When Magic watched basketball as a child, he never imagined he would eventually be playing beside superstar Kareem Abdul-Jabbar.*

interviewed on TV. He directed his words to Kareem. "Big fella, I did it for you," he said. "I know your ankle hurts." Magic grinned his famous grin, "But I want you to get up and dance."

## OUT OF ACTION

Magic was on top of the world. Why not? He'd nailed an MVP award his first year in the pros. He'd stepped into the shoes of a basketball great and filled them better than anyone had dreamed possible. His career was off to a flying start—and then it crashed.

In November 1980, at the beginning of his second season with the Lakers, Magic faced off against the center of the Atlanta Hawks—Tom Burleson, who stands 7 feet 2 inches (218 cm) tall. Suddenly, they both dived for a loose ball. Burleson was wearing an iron knee brace, and as they collided, the brace crunched Magic's left knee. Although it was painful, Magic limped back down court and kept playing.

A few nights later, the Lakers played Dallas. During the action, Tom LaGarde and Magic slammed into each other. Again, Magic's left knee took the brunt of the impact. The following morning when Magic got up, his knee was stiff. However, Dr. Kerlan, the Lakers' team physician, examined it and found no damage.

Magic played against Kansas City the next night. During the game, Magic heard something snap. He went down and couldn't get up. He had to be helped off the court. He was out of the game. Hospital tests showed that his cartilage was badly torn and surgery would be needed to repair it.

## THE DIFFICULT TIME

Magic's parents flew out to lend him their support while he was in the hospital. After the operation, his left leg was in a bulky plaster cast. Nevertheless, the doctors wanted him to walk on his leg to circulate the blood. He was sweating when he stood up. Taking his first step, Magic keeled over and fainted.

Three more days passed before he was able to force himself to walk. He had to wear a plaster cast for three weeks. When it was finally taken off, Magic was shocked. His left leg looked about half as big as his right leg. The muscles were so weak that there seemed to be no strength at all in his leg. Rehabilitating that leg was a long, painful process. It involved outpatient physical therapy at the hospital twice a day, six days a week. Sometimes Magic thought he might never be able to play basketball again.

He went back to Lansing to be with his parents while his knee healed. He sat around, watched television, and was very depressed. Magic missed the banter of the locker room. He longed for the team play, the soaring feeling of a **jump shot**, the rush of exultation after a slam dunk. "It's the most down I've ever been," he said later.

## THE HARD ROAD BACK

Magic's depression lifted when the doctors said he was well enough to start practicing. Pat Riley, then the Lakers' assistant coach, walked him through some easy drills. Then the drills got harder. Magic gritted his teeth and practiced sliding, rebounds, layups, and dunks—the whole catalog of court maneuvers. Retraining his body was a long, grueling experience.

Much later, Magic would comment wryly that it had been a learning experience too. All through junior high, high school, and college, he had never missed a game due to an injury. Now, sitting on the bench and watching the games helplessly was agony for him. But it also forced him to learn patience, which had never been one of his strong points.

It was the end of the season before Magic was able to play again. The Lakers had adapted to his absence and won most of their games without him. It was an adjustment for them, as well as for

Magic, when he returned. He had, after all, missed forty-five consecutive games!

## MAGIC'S BAD SPELL

The first quarter of the first game he played after his injury did not go well for Magic. The first time he passed the ball it went straight into the hands of a player on the opposing team. Then Magic missed the first two shots he took. The second quarter went a little better. His performance was good enough but it wasn't great. It just was not the kind of razzle-dazzle play that had always been associated with Magic Johnson.

The problem was his knee. It felt fine, but Magic couldn't stop himself from protecting it. He was afraid to play too aggressively. He was afraid to **drive** to the rim. For the first time in his basketball career, Magic felt vulnerable.

His loss of confidence worried him as the season came to a close. The Lakers had made it to the 1980–1981 NBA championship playoffs. Their first challenge was against Houston, with a two-out-of-three win required to stay in the competition. The Lakers won the first game and Houston took the second. The third game was crucial. The team that lost would be out of the running.

It was close all the way, despite a really bad performance by Magic. He shot for the basket only thirteen times and eleven of his tries were misses. Finally, it came down to the last quarter. Houston led by one point with fifteen seconds left on the clock. Magic dribbled down court, weaving and looking to feed the ball to Kareem Abdul-Jabbar. But Jabbar was covered, and Magic couldn't pass the ball safely. He drove for the hoop, ran into Houston's Moses Malone, and put up the game-ending shot that could have given the Lakers the series. He missed it.

## THE FANS BOO MAGIC

That was the worst year in Magic's career. The next year, 1982, was better. Magic was back in stride and the Lakers once again nailed the NBA championship. However, that was also the year Lakers fans booed Magic for the first time.

It all started when a feud erupted between Magic and Coach Paul Westhead. The coach had tried to reshape the offensive strategy of the Lakers, but Magic thought it was working pretty well the way it was. The newspapers got hold of an account of the resulting confrontation. The media played it up, exaggerating the whole incident, and making Magic look like a **prima donna**.

Things got worse when the owner of the Lakers, Jerry Buss, announced that he was firing Westhead. The coach had been popular with the fans, and the media made it sound as if Magic might have had something to do with the owner's decision. For several games, every time Magic came out on the court, the fans hooted at him and shouted insults.

## THE BOOS TURN TO CHEERS

The booing stopped not too long after Pat Riley was promoted from assistant coach to coach. He

*Magic Johnson and the new Lakers' coach Pat Riley proved to be a winning combination.*

quickly proved himself with a winning Lakers team. Magic was his key player, and he was doing so well that soon the boos were turning to cheers. Magic got full credit from the fans for his role in leading the Lakers to another NBA championship.

They weren't champions the next year, but they came close. Magic had hit his stride and the fans knew it. He played a major role in the team making the 1983 NBA finals, and nobody blamed him when the 76ers knocked the Lakers out of the running.

Both Magic and the Lakers were still turning in peak performances in 1984. Once again they reached the NBA championship finals. This time, they would be playing the Boston Celtics. Some basketball sportswriters called the game the match of the century. The Lakers' Magic Johnson would face the Celtics' Larry Bird.

# CHAPTER FIVE

# A CHAMPIONSHIP RIVALRY

In his autobiography, Magic wrote about the opening game of the 1984 NBA championship series between the Celtics and the Lakers. "The first time I ever saw Boston Garden," he admitted, "I was shocked at how old and dirty it was." Nevertheless, he thought it was "a great arena for basketball" with perfect lighting—a shooter's court.

Magic's problem was the floor. It was full of loose bolts and dead spots. "I've played on driveways that were smoother," Magic joked. The Celtics were always waiting to pounce when a visiting hoopster dribbled onto a dead spot. "They'd chase you into the corner and steal the ball," claimed Magic.

In general, the Celtics played a rougher, more physical game than the Lakers. The Lakers, like Magic himself, were known for their speed and agility, for quick reflexes, and for fast breaks. The sportswriters, particularly the Boston media, regarded the seven-game match as "blood, sweat, and tears versus glitter and gold."

**"Blood, sweat, and tears versus glitter and gold."**

## A SEESAW SERIES

The focus was on Magic Johnson and Larry Bird, and it was intense. Basketball enthusiasts around the United States were debating which of the two was the better player. The press had built it up into a feud and Magic and Larry, who barely knew each other, had fallen into an attitude of hostility. Their hostility had no basis, except that it seemed to be expected of them.

To a lesser extent, that attitude had rubbed off on the other Lakers and Celtics. In the first game, the Celtics seemed to be bumping and bruising Lakers at every opportunity. Magic remembered the game and the series as the roughest he ever played. Nevertheless, the Lakers led by eighteen points during the first quarter. Magic hit his stride, and the team took their lead from him, beating the Celtics 115–109.

The second game was a different story. With

*The hype created by the media forced Magic and Larry into a feud that spread to the rest of their teammates and to all their fans.*

thirteen seconds left to play, the Celtics intercepted a pass and scored to tie the game. They won it in overtime, 124–121.

The Lakers ruled game three. Game four, however, went into overtime after an attempted pass by Magic was knocked away. The game was tied at 123 when Magic was given two free throws. After he missed both, Bird scored for the Celtics and the win was theirs. The series was tied at two, and the word was that Bird had outplayed Magic.

## ROUGH AND TUMBLE

The fourth game had increased the bitterness of the rivalry between the Celtics and the Lakers. One of the Celtics had gone too far with a vicious foul that sent a Laker crashing to the floor. Players came tumbling off the benches and a big fight almost erupted.

The incident was very much in Magic's mind when they went into game five back in Boston. The city was having a heat wave, and Boston Garden was not air-conditioned. Kareem Abdul-Jabbar had to use an oxygen mask between plays. Tempers were frayed on both sides. It was home court for the Celtics though, and they were more used to the Boston weather. Larry Bird played brilliantly, again outshining Magic. Bird scored fifteen of his twenty shots, and the Celtics walked away with game five.

Game six was back in Los Angeles at the Forum. Revenge for the violence of game four bubbled up. The game was very intense. The Lakers barely managed to pull it out. Now the series was tied 3–3. The final game would be played in Boston.

## THE DECIDING PLAY

Boston fans were enraged by the violence against the Celtics at the Forum. Feelings ran so high that the police had to escort the Lakers from Boston's Logan Airport to their hotel. The team also needed police protection for their entrance into Boston Garden. The boos that greeted them when they took to the court were devastating. The fans' comments were particularly ugly, and Magic was the target of many of them.

The crowd's hostility shook up Magic and the rest of the Lakers. By the end of the third quarter, the Celtics were holding on to a fourteen-point lead. In the fourth quarter, however, the Lakers caught fire and cut the Celtics' lead to three points. There was one minute left to play. Magic had the ball. Teammate James Worthy was in the clear at the basket. Poised to pass, Magic felt the ball jolted from his hands by Celtic Cedric

Maxwell. The Lakers lost the game, and the Celtics won the title.

Magic had not played well. He had scored only five baskets in fourteen tries. In the final moments, he had lost the ball twice, the second time sealing the Celtic victory. Bird, however, as the media was quick to point out, played brilliantly.

In the immediate aftermath of the game, Magic didn't have time to think about that. Despite the Celtics' victory, the Boston fans were still furious with the Lakers. The Los Angeles team was surrounded as they tried to get on the bus that would take them back to their hotel. Fans threw rocks and bottles. Once the Lakers were aboard the bus, the crazed fans smashed the windows. They started rocking the bus, trying to turn it over. Finally the police rescued the Lakers. Things calmed down, and Magic was able to think bitter thoughts about Larry Bird.

## RIVALS BECOME FRIENDS

Magic's feelings were still smoldering when two surprising offers arose that changed Magic's attitude toward Bird. The offers were invitations to do commercials—the first for Amoco gas and the second for Converse sneakers. But these offers were not for Magic alone. The commercials would feature both Magic and Larry Bird.

The first commercial was shot in Los Angeles, the second in French Lick, Indiana, where Larry Bird lived. It was an awkward situation. It included a lot of standing around waiting for the cameras to be set up. Given the rivalry between Bird and Magic, small talk wasn't easy. But after a while, they thawed. They actually had a lot in common.

They talked about basketball, about salaries, about coaches and other players, and about their college years and their families. They talked about the media. Neither of them liked the hype that had built them up as enemies. They were rivals, sure, but they didn't hate each other. As a matter of fact, they now liked each other.

The friendship flourished. Through the years, Magic and Bird sent each other kidding notes and gag gifts. When Magic put on an exhibition game for the United Negro College Fund, Larry Bird participated, even though it was against Celtics policy for their players to perform in charity games.

## THE MEMORIAL DAY MASSACRE

Friendship, however, didn't lessen their fierce competitiveness. Magic liked Larry, but the 1984 defeat by the Celtics still hurt. The end of the 1985 season, though, was payback time. Again, the championship came down to the Lakers ver-

*The rivalry between Magic and Bird resulted in a
lasting friendship that they both treasure.*

sus the Celtics, Magic versus Bird. All season
long, as they piled up victory after victory, the
Lakers had rooted for the Celtics to make the
playoffs. They wanted another shot at them.

Arriving in Boston for the first game of the
1985 NBA battle for the championship, the Lakers were ripe for revenge. They didn't get their
revenge, however. That first game went down in

basketball history as the "Memorial Day Massacre." That's how badly Boston creamed the Lakers.

The Lakers were down, but they weren't out. Pulling themselves together, they managed to eke out a victory against Boston in the second game. Then, back at the Forum in Los Angeles, the Lakers won two out of three games, giving them a 3–2 lead as they went back to Boston for the last two games—if two games were necessary.

They weren't. The Lakers took an early lead in game six and held on to it. The Boston Garden was quiet; the Celtics fans sat stunned and silent as the Lakers won the game—and the series. The Lakers had played so well that the Boston fans actually applauded them when the game was over.

## ONCE AGAIN, THE BIRD

The next season, 1985–1986, was both good and bad for Magic. In the beginning, he was plagued by illness and injuries. He missed the first game when he came down with shingles—a virus that plays havoc with the nervous system. After he recovered from that, he sprained a finger in practice. When that was better, he banged up his knee. Despite these problems, Magic had a good season. He averaged 18.8 points and 12.6 assists per game. Fifty-two percent of his shots went through the hoop to score.

The team did not do as well, though. For the first time since 1982, they did not make the NBA finals. Magic could only watch as the Celtics took the championship four games to two from the Houston Rockets. And he could only grin and be happy for Larry Bird when he was named MVP.

"Wait until next year" has always been the cry of the losing team. This time it came true. In 1987, the Boston Celtics and the Los Angeles Lakers again faced off for the NBA championship. Each team had won the NBA title three times. Each had won one championship at the expense of the other. This series was the tiebreaker, and it was regarded as the ultimate contest between Magic Johnson and Larry Bird.

# CHAPTER SIX

# THE CLIFFHANGER

The first two games of the 1986–1987 season NBA championships were played at the Forum in Los Angeles, and the Lakers won them both hands down. Back in Boston though, Larry Bird took over the court. He was unstoppable. He led the Celtics to a 109–103 victory.

Larry Bird was still hot in game four. At the end of the first half, the Celtics led 55–47. At the end of the third quarter, they led by sixteen points. But in the fourth quarter, Magic came alive. He sank shot after shot. Now the score was tied at ninety-five. But Bird wasn't finished. His hair was a blond blur as he broke through the Lakers' defense play after play. The fans were on their feet cheering Bird. Again, the Celtics gained a lead in the game.

Magic redoubled his efforts. The Lakers cut the lead to only one point, with eight seconds to go in the game. With the clock ticking, Magic took the ball down court. With two seconds to go, he fired the ball at the basket. It was a baby sky-hook—a flashy shot usually associated with Kareem Abdul-Jabbar. A gasp went through the audience as the ball spiraled through the air and dropped clean through the basket just as the buzzer sounded. The Lakers had won game four 107–106.

## THE SLAM DUNK

Game five was played in Los Angeles. The Lakers had home-court advantage, but it did them little good. Magic played well enough, but Bird was unstoppable. The Celtics won by a comfortable 123 to 108. The Lakers were now ahead by only one game.

Oh, that Bird! Magic hated losing, but he couldn't contain his admiration for his rival. Bird was so good that Magic had no choice but to push himself to play better. The better Larry Bird was, the better Magic Johnson was going to have to be.

Magic needed to settle himself down, but he couldn't seem to do that during the first half of game six. He missed seven of the nine shots he took. Bird and the Celtics were ahead by five points at halftime. Magic was back in form in the third period. He started out by zeroing in on a loose ball and driving it down court to score a

*Magic shoots a sky hook over Boston's Danny Ainge during the sixth game of the 1987 NBA finals.*

slam dunk. After that there was no stopping him. Magic scored fourteen points in the third quarter. The Lakers won the game 106–93, and won the championship. And, sweet victory, this time Magic was named MVP.

## ATHLETE OF THE DECADE

Toward the end of 1989, *Sport* magazine was narrowing down the list of those being considered for its Athlete of the Decade award. The finalists included hockey superstar Wayne Gretzky, football

*Magic joyfully rides a championship float as MVP of the 1987 victory over the Boston Celtics.*

quarterback Joe Montana, tennis champion Martina Navratilova, and basketball rivals Larry Bird and Magic Johnson—all top competitors who had given their all to their sport.

None of them, however, had piled up a championship record during the 1980s that could equal Magic's. Over a ten-year period he had led the Lakers to the NBA finals eight times. On five of those occasions, Magic's spectacular court play had propelled them to win the title. "That's winning!" was *Sport* magazine's judgment as it honored Magic with its Athlete of the Decade award.

**"That's winning!"**

In the following year, Magic earned his third regular season MVP award. In 1991, he and the Lakers again became eligible to play in the NBA finals. They would go up against the Chicago Bulls. For the first time, Magic would be facing Michael Jordan.

## HIS AIRNESS, MICHAEL JORDAN

In *My Life*, Magic pointed out that "Michael Jordan can do incredible things, including moves I've never seen before. There's nobody like him." In Magic's opinion, "Michael Jordan might be the most popular athlete ever."

Basketball insiders call him "Air Jordan," or "His Airness." At 6 feet 6 inches (198 cm) and 198 pounds (90 kg), Michael is 3 inches (8 cm) shorter than Magic and 27 pounds (12 kg) lighter. He's also four years younger. From Brooklyn, New York, Jordan used to skip classes in high school to play basketball. When his father found out, he read him the riot act. Michael buckled down to do his schoolwork, but he didn't give up shooting baskets. "Who knows what would have happened if my father hadn't talked to me," Jordan says today.

> **"Michael Jordan can do incredible things, including moves I've never seen before. There's nobody like him."**

His grades might not have been high enough for him to be admitted to North Carolina University, but his skills on the court led to an offer to turn pro with the Chicago Bulls. It was the beginning of a remarkable career. By 1995, he had a 32.2 scoring average—the best ever in professional basketball.

## MAGIC AGAINST AIR

In 1991, Michael Jordan and the Chicago Bulls went up against Magic Johnson and the L.A.

*Michael Jordan is about to steal the ball from Magic during game one of the finals. The Lakers win this game, but the Chicago Bulls end up winning the series.*

Lakers for the NBA championship. Going into the first game, the Lakers were hurting. Kareem Abdul-Jabbar had retired. Magic had been playing brilliantly all season, but the rest of the Lakers weren't quite up to the standard he set. Even so, the Lakers won the first game against Jordan and the Bulls. But that was all. Chicago took the next four straight. Jordan averaged 31.1 points a game for the series and was named MVP.

Some time later, a one-on-one match between Magic Johnson and Michael Jordan was discussed. Both players were eager for the match, and it would certainly have been a high point in basketball history. However, the Players' Association opposed the match and the NBA refused to approve it.

# CHAPTER SEVEN

## A BITTER BLOW

While Magic was at Michigan State, he met Earleatha "Cookie" Kelly, a young woman who was working her way through college. She had been a cheerleader in high school. Mutual friends introduced them at a disco, and Magic was immediately attracted to her. He asked for her phone number, and she gave it to him.

It was the beginning of a romance that would last. Magic dated many women during that time, but he always came back to Cookie. Sometimes they had arguments and fights, and sometimes they broke up. But in the end, Magic and Cookie always got back together again. They were in love.

During one of their breakups, Magic had an affair with an old friend, Melissa Mitchell. She became pregnant. Magic was only twenty-one years old when he became a father. He wasn't ready for the responsibility, but he met it as well as he could. He provided money, and he kept in contact with Melissa and their son, Andre. He has tried hard over the years to be a good father to his son.

Cookie knew about Andre. She and Magic had often been apart over the eight years since college, and she had expected him to date other women.

*Magic and Cookie arrive in style at the 1999 Essence Awards in New York.*

Even so, Cookie and Magic couldn't seem to stay away from each other. Then, early in 1991, Magic asked Cookie to marry him, and she accepted. The ceremony took place on September 14, 1991. Magic has called it "one of the happiest days of my life."

**"One of the happiest days of my life."**

## THE SHOCK: HIV POSITIVE

A few weeks after the wedding, Magic had a routine physical examination that included a blood test. On October 25, he was in Salt Lake City for an exhibition game between the Lakers and the Utah Jazz when he received a call from Dr. Michael Mellman, the Lakers' team doctor. The doctor asked Magic to fly back to Los Angeles right away.

Back in Los Angeles, Dr. Mellman sat Magic down. He had the results of the blood test Magic had taken. "You tested positive for HIV, the virus that causes AIDS," he told Magic. Magic was stunned. He thought AIDS was a disease that only affected gay men and drug addicts. He really knew little about it at that time. But he was going to learn.

**"You tested positive for HIV, the virus that causes AIDS."**

*Magic enjoys bringing his oldest son Andre to some of the big events.*

## WHAT *IS* AIDS?

Magic learned that AIDS is caused by a virus. The initials stand for **A**cquired **I**mmuno**d**eficiency **S**yndrome. The name means that the virus stops the immune system—the body's defense against disease—from doing its job. So a person with

AIDS has little protection against diseases and infections.

The virus that causes AIDS is called the Human Immunodeficiency Virus Type 1 (HIV-1). It enters the bloodstream and destroys certain white blood cells that are necessary for the immune system to work properly.

When people are diagnosed as HIV positive— having the HIV-1 virus, as Magic does—it does not mean they will get AIDS immediately. Most people with HIV-1 get AIDS eventually, but "eventually" can sometimes mean twenty years or more. The average time between contracting HIV and show- ing the symptoms of AIDS is eight to eleven years. With the new drugs that are now being developed, doctors look forward to ridding the body of HIV.

## HOW PEOPLE GET HIV

Most people who are HIV positive look and feel healthy, just as Magic does. The virus can remain inactive for long periods of time. But these people can infect others. Over the years, there has been much confusion about how the virus can be passed from one person to another. It is contained in bodily fluids, but it cannot be transmitted by sneezing, tears, or saliva. The virus is passed only through blood and semen.

The most common ways of getting the virus are through sexual intercourse or by sharing hypodermic needles used to inject drugs. When the AIDS epidemic first broke out around 1981, most victims were gay males. A few years later, it became clear that the HIV-1 virus was spreading among drug users. These were originally the two main groups at risk for developing AIDS. Magic is not gay, and he has never used illegal drugs. He had contracted the disease through unprotected sex with a female partner.

## MAGIC TELLS HIS WIFE

Since 1989, two years before Magic was diagnosed HIV positive, AIDS has been spread mainly through heterosexual sex. Since then, some 90 percent of new AIDS cases have been traced to heterosexual intercourse. And today, the people most at risk are between thirteen and nineteen years of age.

The first thing that concerned Magic after he learned of his condition was his wife, Cookie. He was afraid he might have passed the virus to her. The doctor said that Cookie would have to be tested. Before she could be tested though, Magic would have to tell her that he was HIV positive. It was the hardest thing Magic has ever had to do.

When he told Cookie, she cried, but her first concern was for him, not for herself. She thought the diagnosis meant that Magic was going to die soon. After that, her main concern—and Magic's too—was their unborn baby. They had found out only a short time before that Cookie was pregnant. There was a chance that the baby could be HIV positive.

## NOT JUST A GAY DISEASE

A few days later, Cookie's blood was tested to see if she had the HIV virus. Fortunately, the test came back negative. She was fine, and so was the baby. But she would have to be tested again and again. "It can take a while before the virus shows up in the tests," the doctor told them. The risk was small, but real.

Magic had begun taking AZT, a drug that was proving most effective in fighting HIV. It was known to have some side effects—headaches, nausea, diarrhea—but Magic went on playing for a while. Then it became obvious that he couldn't continue. On November 7, 1991, he called a press conference.

"Because of the HIV virus . . . " he told the reporters, "I will have to retire from the Lakers today." He also wanted to make his condition clear, "I do not have the AIDS disease." He announced his intention to "become a

**"Because of the HIV virus . . . I will have to retire from the Lakers today."**

spokesman for the fight against the HIV virus." He was committed to educating young people about the disease.

The announcement was a bombshell. It changed the way people thought about AIDS. "It can happen to everybody," Magic had said. By 1998, it was widely recognized that "when basketball superstar Magic Johnson announced in 1991 that he had contracted the AIDS virus, the feeling spread quickly that anyone, not just particular groups of people, could be at risk."

**"It can happen to everybody."**

*Magic announces his retirement from professional basketball at a press conference in 1991.*

# THE CRUSADE AGAINST HIV-AIDS

On June 4, 1992, Cookie and Magic had a healthy baby boy. Earvin Johnson III did not have HIV. Neither he nor his mother showed any signs of being at risk. The birth of his son was the high point in what had been a busy and exciting time for Magic. It had begun less than a week after he announced his retirement. John Sununu, chief of staff to President George Bush, had contacted Magic's press agent, Lon Rosen, and asked Magic to join the National Commission on AIDS.

When the news leaked, a reporter asked Rosen if Magic wouldn't just be window dressing for the commission. "Magic Johnson won't be a photo opportunity for anybody," was Rosen's reply. When the comment found its way into the papers, Sununu became furious because it accused the commission of using Magic. It looked like the invitation for Magic to join the commission might be withdrawn.

## A LETTER FROM THE PRESIDENT

Magic felt badly about the controversy. To him it seemed like no more than a misunderstanding. Nevertheless, he hesitated to make a decision until it was clear that he was still wanted. He got his answer when he received a letter from President George Bush. The president wrote, "I do not want you to feel that you are being used in any way. I do want you to know on a very personal basis that I respect you, admire you, and hope that you will be able to join the commission."

Magic replied that he would consider it an honor to join the National Commission on AIDS. He also expressed his intention to be an "independent voice" on the commission, and to work to educate African-Americans and young people in particular about AIDS. On January 14, 1992, Magic attended his first meeting with the commission.

## SHOW ME THE MONEY

What Magic learned at that meeting was very upsetting. He learned that nine times as many black women as white women in the United States had AIDS. He found out that for every female white adolescent who had AIDS, there were twenty-nine African-American girls who had the disease. Commission statistics showed him that at the time ten million people worldwide had the HIV virus.

Magic also learned that the Bush administration had been holding back on providing the necessary funds to deal with the disease. Many members of the commission felt that AIDS was already an epidemic. Without the money to fight the epidemic, an enormous disaster could break out.

Magic wrote to the president. He was very specific. He asked the federal government to provide $400 million for AIDS research in 1992 and $500 million in 1993. He requested $300 million for treatment in 1992 and $600 million in 1993. He asked for a change in policy so that **Medicaid** would fund treatment for people with HIV-1, not only those with AIDS. The estimated cost was $500 million for 1993. The estimated savings was millions of lives and, ultimately, billions of dollars.

President Bush wrote to Magic thanking him for his letter, but nothing happened. The money was not forthcoming despite an editorial in *The New York Times* saying that Magic "was right on the mark when he criticized the president for hanging back in the battle against this deadly disease." Then, on June 25, 1992, the National Commission on AIDS issued a statement criticizing the Bush administration for its failure to fight the AIDS epidemic.

## THE MAGIC JOHNSON FOUNDATION

Magic Johnson resigned from the commission on September 25. "I cannot in good conscience continue to serve on a commission whose important work is so utterly ignored by your administration," he said in his letter to President Bush. "I am disappointed that you have dropped the ball."

> **"I cannot in good conscience continue to serve on a commission whose important work is so utterly ignored by your administration."**

Leaving the commission did not mean that Magic was dropping out of the battle against AIDS. In December 1991, he had formed the Magic Johnson Foundation, Inc., a nonprofit organization designed "to carry forth a positive message regarding HIV-AIDS to as many people as possible." Magic continued to give interviews, do television shows, and meet with groups of children in an effort to raise public awareness about

HIV and AIDS. His efforts were part of a calculated campaign to reverse the spread of the disease.

Magic organized exhibition games, fashion shows, circuses, and other functions, with the proceeds going to the fight against AIDS. The foundation funneled money in the form of grants to many small organizations involved in the struggle. Eventually, partnerships were formed with companies such as the Levi Strauss Foundation and AT&T to raise and distribute money to battle AIDS.

*Magic hosts a television special on Nickelodeon to answer children's questions about HIV and AIDS.*

*Local school students join Magic at a Levi's store in New York to ask questions and help promote HIV-AIDS education.*

## THE HARDHEADED BUSINESSMAN

Magic started the foundation that bears his name with his own money. By the time he retired in 1991, he had already become a multimillionaire. His hardheaded attitude toward his financial affairs had been formed as a boy when he was inspired by the successful African-American businessmen whose offices he had cleaned in Lansing.

*Magic attained the executive desk he dreamed about as a boy and became more successful than he ever imagined.*

From the beginning, Magic's salary was high, and he saved a lot of that money. In 1989, he had invested his savings in a T-shirt business. He got a license from the NBA to sell T-shirts with team pictures on them, as well as pictures of star players. He made a similar agreement with the National Football League (NFL), then with the National Hockey League (NHL), and the National Collegiate Athletic Association (NCAA). Today, he has invested his profits from the T-shirt sales in many other enterprises.

## THE COMEBACK THAT FAILED

Magic had announced his retirement in November 1991, but as it turned out, he wasn't finished with basketball. He was named to the 1992 NBA All-Star Team, and he wouldn't back out on that commitment. He racked up twenty-five points in

*Magic goes for a layup during the 1992 NBA All-Star Game. With twenty-five points, nine assists, and five rebounds, he was named the game's MVP.*

the game, had nine assists, and five rebounds. He was named the game's Most Valuable Player.

He had also been picked for the 1992 United States Olympic team. It was the first time players in the NBA had been granted permission to play for the United States. It was a new kind of triumph for Magic when he and the team returned from the games in Barcelona, Spain, with the Olympic gold medal for basketball.

His success in those games gave Magic second thoughts about retiring. In late 1992, he announced that he was going to make a comeback. But he wasn't prepared for the way some of the other players in the NBA reacted to the news.

"What if he sweats or bleeds on another player?" one player worried. "Isn't AIDS contagious?" asked another, unaware that although Magic was HIV positive, he did not have AIDS. Still another was concerned about Magic's health. "Won't he shorten his life by playing?" he wondered. Many of the players had mistaken ideas about Magic's condition. In a way, their worries reflected the attitudes of many Americans who were not accurately informed about HIV or AIDS.

## TIES TO THE LAKERS

Magic did play briefly at the end of 1992, but the concern that he might transmit HIV to another player during a game increased. He was not comfortable on the court and quit playing after a few games.

Basketball was still important to him though. When the National Broadcasting Company (NBC) made him an offer to comment on Bulls–Lakers games at the Forum, Magic jumped at the chance. He and Mike Fratello alternated with comments, while Dick Enberg delivered the play-by-play. "The hardest part," Magic wrote later, "was trying to be objective. . . . It was difficult to criticize my teammates, but sometimes I had to."

**"The hardest part, was trying to be objective. . . . It was difficult to criticize my teammates, but sometimes I had to."**

At the end of the 1993–1994 season, Magic filled in as a coach for the Lakers. In 1994, he bought a share in the team that he would later sell back. It was more than just a business venture. Magic would always regard the Lakers as a family.

Throughout these years, Magic was continuing his efforts to educate the public about HIV and AIDS. Praise for his effort came from many directions. He was regarded as the most effective spokesperson in the United States for AIDS awareness. He played a major role in changing the attitudes of Americans about the disease.

## CHANGED ATTITUDES

That change in attitudes was most visible among NBA basketball players. In 1992, the idea of Magic playing had generated fear, but by 1996, most players knew that their chance of catching HIV from Magic during a game was very low— approximately one in eighty-five million. "It's not like we're going to have unprotected sex with Magic," pointed out Charles Barkley of the Phoenix Suns. "We're just going to play basketball, so I think we'll be okay." Dennis Rodman of the Chicago Bulls put it more bluntly. "Who cares if he's got HIV, measles, cancer, whatever? I'm going to slam him anyway!"

> **"Who cares if he's got HIV, measles, cancer, whatever? I'm going to slam him anyway!"**

Most heartening to Magic was the comment of Karl "The Mailman" Malone of the Utah Jazz. Malone had been highly disapproving of Magic's attempt at a comeback in 1992. He had openly expressed the fear that many players felt. Now he admitted he had been wrong. "I have no problem playing against him, absolutely not," was his response to Magic's 1996 return. "We're more knowledgeable now."

## THE 1996 COMEBACK

Magic had, of course, played a major role in making players more knowledgeable. Now he was about to show them that neither HIV nor his absence from basketball had diminished his skills as a player. On January 30, 1996, he played with the Lakers against the Golden State Warriors. He scored nineteen points. He also had ten assists and eight rebounds. The Lakers won 128–118.

*Magic was embraced by his teammates when he made another comeback to professional basketball in 1996.*

On February 2, the Lakers took on the Chicago Bulls and Dennis Rodman. The top Bull was as good as his word. Magic scored fifteen points and had three assists, but it wasn't enough. It was Rodman's day. The Bulls beat the Lakers 99–84.

Two days later, the Lakers took on the Utah Jazz. Magic faced off against Karl "The Mailman" Malone—the player whose comments had hurt so much four years earlier. Magic had warm feelings toward Malone now, but that didn't keep him from scoring twenty-one points, seven rebounds, and six assists to lead the Lakers to a 110–103 victory.

At the end of the season, Magic retired again. He recognized that either the HIV virus, or the drugs he was taking to fight it, were making him feel physically weaker. It was a minor effect, but as an athlete he couldn't ignore it.

In October 1996, in honor of the NBA's fiftieth anniversary celebration, the association announced the fifty greatest players in the history of the league. Magic Johnson was among those named.

Magic would miss playing basketball, but there were many other things to keep him busy. He had many business interests and a deal was in the making for him to have his own syndicated show, *The Magic Hour*, on late-night television. The show premiered to mixed reviews in June 1998, and was canceled in August.

*Magic enjoys interviewing guest Arnold Schwarzenegger at the opening of his new talk show* The Magic Hour.

Most important to Magic—other than his family, which now includes a daughter named Elisa—is his ongoing AIDS and HIV awareness campaign. That, and a longtime devotion to a variety of charities with which he has been involved for years, take up most of his time. He is an athlete and a businessman, but most of all,

Magic Johnson is a person who believes strongly that he has an obligation toward other human beings. As he always has, Magic continues to act on that obligation.

*Magic cherishes spending time with his wife, Cookie, and his children, Elisa (left) and Earvin Jr.*

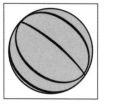

# TELLING IT LIKE IT IS

Magic Johnson has been, and still is, one of the most admired athletes in the world. His basketball skills—his endurance and agility—have earned him that admiration. Nobody who follows the sport can doubt that he deserves it.

He has also earned respect as a businessman. His ability to recognize an opportunity and to put in the hard work needed to develop it has made him wealthy. Magic's business philosophy is clear—all business ventures must have a redeeming social value. Most recently, Magic has devoted his time to his growing business empire—Magic Johnson Enterprises (MJE) in Beverly Hills, California.

MJE has many divisions, including the Johnson Development Corporation, Magic Johnson T's, Magic Johnson All-Star Camps, Magic Johnson Theatres, and his most recent project, Magic

Johnson Entertainment. The Johnson Development Corporation partnered with SONY Pictures to open Magic Johnson Theatres in Los Angeles, Atlanta, Houston, and many other big cities across the United States.

"I think that's the best example I can set for black kids in this country who see playing sports as the only way they can make it," says Magic. "I'd like them to see that blacks can not only make money playing, but also make money in other

*Magic joins the employees of Magic Johnson Theatres for a promotional photo shoot at the refreshment stand.*

ways. We can be businessmen too." Magic wants young people to understand that not everybody can be a successful athlete, and he hopes that his success in the world beyond basketball will make him a more realistic role model for them.

> **"I'd like them to see that blacks can not only make money playing, but also make money in other ways. We can be businessmen too."**

## GETTING THE MESSAGE OUT

The crusade he has led for HIV-AIDS awareness has brought Magic respect and praise from many areas. More than anyone else, Magic has changed the attitude of the public toward this disease. He has made people understand that it is not a disease affecting only gays, but that we are all at risk. Through his foundation, he has raised money for research, for the development of new drugs, and for treatment programs.

Magic has been most effective in getting the message out to young people. He has consistently visited inner-city schools across the country. He concentrates on them because of the higher rate of AIDS among African-American teenagers.

From psychologists, he has learned that the

best time to inform young people about AIDS is before they reach their teens. Magic had some messages for them. He told them bluntly that it was best to hold off on sex until they were adults. Sex carries with it responsibilities and consequences, and it requires mature judgment.

## MAGIC'S CONTROVERSIAL BOOK

Nevertheless, Magic is realistic. His aim is to prevent the spread of HIV infections and AIDS. He recognizes that many young people will have sex in their teens. To them, Magic stresses the dangers of unprotected sex. He is frank about how he was infected with HIV. "It happened because I had unprotected sex," he tells them.

Magic has written a book about AIDS for teens. *What You Can Do to Avoid AIDS* was published in 1992 by Times Books, a division of Random House. The paperback version is inexpensive because Magic wanted it to be affordable for young people, and because he thought a paperback would have the widest distribution.

The book is candid and direct. Magic thought it was more important to get the message across than to avoid offending some people. Kmart and Walgreen's refused to carry the book because store officials thought it was too graphic. Other chains did carry the book, however, and it has enjoyed steady sales. All the profits go to the Magic Johnson Foundation, which uses the money to fund a variety of projects to fight HIV and AIDS.

## A DROP IN TEENAGE SEX

It is widely recognized that Magic has played a key role in changing teenage sexual behavior. He has not been alone in this campaign, but his has been one of the best-known and most respected

*Magic speaks about the importance of reading at Garfield High School in Seattle, Washington.*

voices. In his view, progress has been slow—too slow perhaps—but it has occurred.

According to a May 1997 survey quoted in *The New York Times*, sexual activity among U.S. teenagers had dropped for the first time in twenty years. Most importantly, from Magic's point of view, is the increased use of condoms among those having sex for the first time. According to the survey, three out of four teens are using protection now, an 11 percent gain over the late 1980s survey. This has been reflected in a sharp decline in the number of teenage girls having babies.

### COMRADES

Another message Magic is eager to get across concerns tolerance. "I'm not a hero because I got HIV," Magic stresses in *What You Can Do to Avoid AIDS*. But, he adds, "I didn't get HIV because I was a 'bad' person or a 'dirty' one or someone who 'deserved' it for whatever reason. I got HIV because I had unprotected sex."

> **"I didn't get HIV because I was a 'bad' person or a 'dirty' one or someone who 'deserved' it for whatever reason. I got HIV because I had unprotected sex."**

In an interview with Arsenio Hall shortly after Magic's announcement that he was

HIV positive, he was asked if he had caught the HIV virus through having a homosexual relationship. Magic replied that he was "far from being a homosexual," and the audience applauded. That made Magic feel awkward. Although he is not gay, he works with many gay people and organizations in the fight against HIV-AIDS, and he respects them.

He also understands their anger. For a long time they were fighting the battle alone. The general public considered it a "gay disease" and some even viewed it as a punishment for gay behavior. But Magic, of all people, knew that wasn't true. Today, in the life-and-death battle to stop the spread of AIDS, he is proud to call people with many different lifestyles his comrades. "The bond is there," says Magic. "I'm in the trenches with them, and I'm fighting beside them."

**"The bond is there, I'm in the trenches with them, and I'm fighting beside them."**

## GIVING SOMETHING BACK

Many people don't realize it, but Magic was active in the fight against HIV-AIDS before he learned that he was HIV positive. Helping to raise money to fight the disease was only one of the many charities with which Magic has long been involved. He was raised to believe that when life is good to you, you have a duty to give something back.

This has been his philosophy since his earliest days in the NBA. He has performed free in exhibition games and appeared at benefits to raise money for such charitable organizations as the Muscular Dystrophy Association and the City of Hope Medical Research Center. Also, flashing his irresistible smile, he has persuaded other star players to join him in raising money for charity.

Every year he sponsors a celebrity golf tournament for the American Heart Association that raises some $200,000. According to Magic, some of the basketball greats who enter the tournament compete just as fiercely on the golf course as they do driving for the rim.

Magic has also devoted a great deal of time and effort to raising money for the United Negro College Fund (UNCF). He considers a college education the best tool an African-American young person can have in climbing the ladder to success in today's world. The money Magic raises for the fund goes to help African-American students in forty-one colleges in the United States. Each summer, Magic persuades top NBA players to join him at the Great Western Forum for "Midsummer Night's Magic," a special exhibition game with the proceeds going to the UNCF. The event has raised more than $10 million.

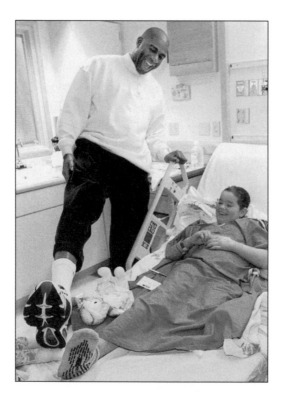

*Magic visits with Felicia Fusco at Rainbow Babies and Children's Hospital in December 1999. Felicia, who is nine years old, is recovering from surgery to remove a tumor from her lung.*

The Magic Johnson Foundation also funds the Taylor Michaels Scholarship Program, which "provides support for deserving inner-city high school students who have a strong potential for academic achievement, but lack the social or economic support necessary for them to achieve their potential and reach their goals." Also, Magic Johnson Technology Centers provides computer training and access to low-income minorities in inner-city areas, such as South Central Los Angeles; Harlem, New York; Cleveland, Ohio; Atlanta, Georgia; and Houston, Texas.

Magic Bowl is an annual kickoff party that celebrates the Super Bowl. The world's biggest celebrities and athletes attend the many activities. This event is a fund-raiser that benefits the Atlanta University Center, Clark Atlanta University, Morehouse College, Morris Brown University, and Spelman College.

Magic's Youth Entrepreneurial Project gives inner-city young people the opportunity to intern at one of Magic's many companies. Some internships include work in entertainment and sports, commercial development, film and television, and concert promotion.

## BE THE BEST YOU CAN BE

Helping other people is something Magic feels strongly about. "Frankly, I can't understand why some players don't get involved in charities," he has written. "Don't they remember that somebody helped them out? Lots of people helped me and I won't forget them."

Most of all, he devotes himself to children. He wants to give the kind of guidance that will help them steer a clear course through a world that is often confusing and even dangerous. There is love in his heart for all children, but he knows that

**"Lots of people helped me and I won't forget them."**

for many of the children of minorities life is more difficult.

Magic's message is frank—"Growing up today is hard." He tells them that there were no gangs,

*Magic has devoted his life not only to his own children, but to all children who need guidance growing up.*

or guns, or much in the way of drugs when he was their age. Today's youngsters have to deal with drugs and AIDS and many other issues.

"But you can't let yourself give up," Magic declares. "If you get your education, you can look beyond." He warns them to pay no attention to those who put down their ambitions and dreams. "A lot of people doubted me too," he reminds them. His message is, have faith in yourself. Every one of you, he insists, can be the best that you can be!

> **"But you can't let yourself give up, if you get your education, you can look beyond."**

*Both Magic and Blayze McDonald, an eleven-year-old from Michigan, agree to give it their best shot.*

## CHRONOLOGY

| | |
|---|---|
| 1959 | Earvin Johnson Jr. is born on August 14. |
| 1974 | Johnson plays basketball for Everett High School; Fred Stabley of the *Lansing State Journal* nicknames him "Magic." |
| 1977–1978 | Led by Magic, the Michigan State Spartans win the Big Ten Conference for the first time in nineteen years. Magic is the only college freshman named to the All-American team. |
| 1978–1979 | Facing Larry Bird for the first time, Magic leads the Spartans to an NCAA championship. |
| 1979 | In June, Magic is the first pick in the draft by the Los Angeles Lakers. |
| 1980 | Replacing Kareem Abdul-Jabbar in the sixth game of the NBA championship series, Magic leads the Lakers to victory and is named series Most Valuable Player. |

| | |
|---|---|
| 1980–1981 | Magic is injured early in the season and misses forty-five games. |
| 1982 | The Lakers win the NBA championship. |
| 1984 | Magic and the Lakers lose the NBA championship playoff series to Larry Bird and the Boston Celtics. |
| 1985 | The Celtics lose the NBA championship playoff series to the Lakers. |
| 1987 | Again, the Lakers beat the Celtics for the NBA championship. |
| 1989 | *Sport* magazine gives Magic their Athlete of the Decade award. |
| 1990 | Magic earns his third MVP award. |
| 1991 | Magic and Earleatha "Cookie" Kelly are wed on September 14. Magic is informed he is HIV positive on October 24, and announces his retirement from professional basketball on November 7. In December, Magic forms the Magic Johnson Foundation to raise public awareness about HIV-AIDS. |
| 1992 | On June 4, Cookie gives birth to their son, Earvin Johnson III. Magic and the Dream Team win an Olympic gold medal. Criticizing the administration for lack of support, Magic resigns from the National Commission on AIDS on September 25. Magic tries to make a comeback in the NBA, but gives up because of other players' fear of catching AIDS. *What You Can* |

*Do to Avoid AIDS* by Magic Johnson is published.

1994     Magic fills in as a coach for the Lakers, and then becomes a part owner of the team.

1996     Magic sells back his share in the Lakers to make a comeback playing for them, but then retires again. Magic is named one of the fifty greatest players in NBA history.

1998     Magic's late-night television show, *The Magic Hour,* premieres in June, but is canceled in August.

2000     Magic continues building his business empire, Magic Johnson Enterprises, and maintains his legacy of charities and community activities with the Magic Johnson Foundation. He lives in California with his wife Cookie and their children.

**NCAA—Michigan State University Spartans—** 1979 All America First Team, NCAA Division One Championship, and Tournament MVP

| Season | No. of Games Played | Points Per Game | Total Points Scored | Field Goal % | Free Throw % | Rebounds | Assists |
|--------|------|------|------|------|------|------|------|
| 1977–1978 | 30 | 17 | 511 | 45.8 | 78.5 | 237 | 222 |
| 1978–1979 | 32 | 17.1 | 548 | 46.8 | 84.2 | 234 | 269 |
| **Totals** | **62** | **17.1** | **1059** | **46.3** | **81.6** | **471** | **491** |

**NBA—Los Angeles Lakers**—NBA record for career assists; MVP 1987, 1989, 1990; All-Star Game MVP 1990, 1992

| Season | No. of Games Played | Points Per Game | Total Points Scored | Field Goal % | Free Throw % | Rebounds | Assists |
|--------|------|------|------|------|------|------|------|
| 79–80 | 77 | 18.0 | 1387 | 53.0 | 81.0 | 596 | 563 |
| 80–81 | 37 | 21.6 | 798 | 53.2 | 76.0 | 320 | 317 |
| 81–82 | 78 | 18.6 | 1447 | 53.7 | 76.0 | 751 | 743 |
| 82–83 | 79 | 16.8 | 1326 | 54.8 | 80.0 | 683 | 829 |
| 83–84 | 67 | 17.6 | 1178 | 56.5 | 81.0 | 491 | 875 |
| 84–85 | 77 | 18.3 | 1406 | 56.1 | 84.3 | 476 | 968 |
| 85–86 | 72 | 18.8 | 1354 | 52.6 | 87.1 | 426 | 907 |
| 86–87 | 80 | 23.9 | 1909 | 52.2 | 84.8 | 504 | 977 |
| 87–88 | 72 | 19.6 | 1408 | 49.2 | 85.3 | 449 | 858 |
| 88–89 | 77 | 22.5 | 1730 | 50.9 | 91.1 | 607 | 988 |
| 89–90 | 79 | 22.3 | 1765 | 48.0 | 89.0 | 522 | 907 |
| 90–91 | 79 | 19.4 | 1531 | 47.7 | 90.6 | 551 | 989 |
| 95–96 | 32 | 14.6 | 468 | 46.6 | 85.6 | 183 | 220 |
| **Totals** | **906** | **19.5** | **17707** | **52.0** | **84.8** | **6559** | **10141** |

# GLOSSARY

**AIDS (*A*cquired *I*mmuno*d*eficiency Syndrome)** a life-threatening disease of the human immune system that is caused by infection with the human immunodeficiency virus. HIV is transmitted through blood and bodily secretions.

**assist** a pass to a teammate who then scores a basket

**drive** an aggressive dribble toward the basket

**field goal** a basket scored while the ball is in play

**free throw** a penalty shot from behind the free-throw line that is taken after being fouled by an opponent

**HIV (*H*uman *I*mmunodeficiency *V*irus)** the virus that causes AIDS

**HIV positive** carrying the human immunodeficiency virus, but not necessarily having AIDS

**jump ball** the ball thrown in the air by the referee to start or restart play

**jump shot**   shooting at the basket while both feet are off the ground

**layup**   a shot near the basket usually made by playing the ball off the backboard

**matchup**   opposing players guarding each other throughout a game

**Medicaid**   financial aid funded by the government for those unable to afford regular medical services

**one-on-one**   a basketball match between two players in which they alternately play offense and defense

**options**   the entire range of offensive moves

**point guard**   the player who organizes the attacking play

**prima donna**   an extremely conceited or undisciplined person

**rebound**   a ball that is caught after a missed shot bounces off the rim, or the backboard

**slam dunk**   when a player jumps and pushes the ball into the basket from above

**steal**   a ball taken by force from an opponent

**tip-off**   a jump ball

**turnover**   when a team loses the ball to the opposing team

# A NOTE ON SOURCES

The primary sources for the author's research were two autobiographies by Earvin Magic Johnson, *Magic's Touch*, written with Roy S. Johnson (Reading, MA: Addison-Wesley Publishing Company, Inc., 1989), and *My Life*, written with William Novak (New York: Fawcett Crest, 1992). Other sources were *Magic Johnson: Hero On and Off Court* by Bill Gutman (Brookfield, CT: The Millbrook Press, 1994); *Basketball's Smiling Superstar: Magic Johnson* by Rick L. Johnson (New York: Dillon Press, 1992); *The Courage of Magic Johnson* by Peter Pascarelli (New York: Bantam Books, 1992); and *Magic Johnson: Champion with a Cause* by Keith Elliot Greenberg (Minneapolis: Lerner, 1996).

*The Kids' World Almanac of Basketball* by Dan Gutman (Mahwah, NJ: World Almanac Books, 1995) was particularly helpful in evaluating the careers of Magic Johnson and his contemporaries. Articles in *Esquire* (April 1990), *Jet* (May 6, 1991), and *Sport*

(October 1989) magazines were also helpful, as was background material from the sports section of various issues of *The New York Times*. A *Times* article (3/4/98, p. B3) on Magic's business activities provided insight into that aspect of his life.

Information on AIDS and HIV is based on material in *What You Can Do to Avoid AIDS* by Earvin Magic Johnson (New York: Times Books, 1992); *Compton's Interactive Encyclopedia* (1998); and the *Grolier Multimedia Encyclopedia* (1998). Information was updated from articles in *The New York Times* (5/2/97, 5/1/98, and 6/24/98), and from data provided by the Centers for Disease Control and Prevention's National AIDS Clearinghouse.

# FOR MORE INFORMATION

## BOOKS

Gutman, Bill. *Magic Johnson: Hero On and Off Court*. Brookfield, Conn.: The Millbrook Press, 1994.

Johnson, Earvin Magic and Roy S. Johnson. *Magic's Touch*. Reading, Mass.: Addison-Wesley Publishing Company, Inc., 1989.

Johnson, Earvin Magic with William Novak. *My Life*. New York: Fawcett Crest, 1992.

Johnson, Earvin Magic. *What You Can Do to Avoid AIDS*. New York: Times Books, 1992.

Mullin, Chris. *The Young Basketball Player: A Young Enthusiast's Guide to Basketball*. New York: A Dorling Kindersley Book, 1995.

Stewart, Mark. *Basketball: A History of Hoops*. Danbury, Conn.: Franklin Watts, 1998.

Withers, Tom. *Basketball: How to Play the All-Star Way*. Austin, Tex.: Raintree Steck-Vaughn Publishers, 1994.

## ORGANIZATIONS

**Basketball Congress International Inc.**
1210 E. Indian School Rd.
Phoenix, AZ 85014

**Centers for Disease Control and National AIDS Hotline**
A telephone service; address confidential
Phone: 1-800-342-AIDS
Phone for Spanish: 1-800-344-SIDA
Phone for the deaf and hearing impaired: 1-800-243-7889

**Magic Johnson Foundation**
600 Corporate Point, Suite 1080
Culver City, CA 90230

**National Basketball Players Association**
1700 Broadway, 14th floor
New York, NY 10019

**Teens Teaching AIDS Prevention**
A telephone service staffed by teenagers to educate and help peers; address confidential
1-800-234-8336
4:00 P.M. to 8:00 P.M. Central time, weekdays only

**United States Institute of Amateur Athletics**
P.O. Box 564
National City, CA 91951

# WEBSITES

## American Social Health Association
*http://www.ashastd.org*
Displays a variety of information on health, focusing on sexually transmitted diseases, and includes contact information for hotlines and support groups

## The Basketball Hall of Fame
*http://www.hoophall.com*
Includes information on awards, events, exhibits, basketball history, and more

## CDC National Prevention Information Network
*http://www.cdcnpin.org*
Includes up-to-date news, information, and research on HIV, sexually transmitted diseases, and tuberculosis

## Magic Johnson Foundation
*http://www.magicjohnson.org*
This official website includes news about Magic's businesses, charities, and community activities, as well as biographical information.

## NBA.com
*http://www.nba.com*
Official site of the National Basketball Association

**Women's National Basketball Association**

*http://www.wnba.com*

The official site of the WNBA—includes news, features, statistics, merchandise, and much more

# INDEX

## ABOUT THE AUTHOR

Ted Gottfried has written more than fifty books, both fiction and nonfiction. Among those for young adults are Police Under Fire; Homelessness: Whose Problem Is It?; James Baldwin: A Voice from Harlem; Alan Turing: Architect of the Computer Age; Eleanor Roosevelt: First Lady of the Twentieth Century; Alexander Fleming: Discoverer of Penicillin; and Capital Punishment: The Death Penalty Debate. Mr. Gottfried has taught writing at New York University, Baruch College, and other institutions. He and his wife Harriet, an Assistant Coordinator of the Office of Community Outreach Services for the New York Public Library, live in New York City.